CRITTER CUISINE

Photography by Al Clayton
Text and Styling by Mary Ann Clayton

LONGSTREET PRESS
Atlanta, Georgia

Published by
LONGSTREET PRESS, INC.
A subsidiary of Cox Newspapers,
A division of Cox Enterprises, Inc.
2140 Newmarket Parkway
Suite 118
Marietta, GA 30067

Printed in the United States of America

2nd printing 1993

Library of Congress Catalog Card Number: 92-71787

ISBN 1-56352-023-0

This book was printed by Horowitz/Rae Book Manufacturers, Inc., Fairfield, New Jersey.
The text was set in Bernhart Modern.
Color separations by Graphics International, Inc., Atlanta, Georgia.

Book design by Jill Dible.
Jacket design by Amy Wheless.

Nothing was sacrificed for the sake of this book. As for the recipes, the authors take no responsibility for their authenticity or reliability. Neither do the editors or the publisher.

CONTENTS

PREFACE

This book is intended as a spoof of "gourmet" mania, but it is also meant to be a thought-provoking look at cultural food prejudices. Why would a sophisticated diner lick, with relish, the last traces of garlic-buttered snails (escargots) from his lips but look with disdain at a platter of tadpoles prepared in the same manner? ◆ Why would a person who, with great pride, tracks, kills and dresses out a possum for Sunday dinner be repulsed by a platter of raw fish (sushi)? Perhaps a little humor about our eating preferences can unite us in the celebration of our individual and cultural diversities.

ACKNOWLEDGMENTS

We deeply appreciate the many friends, family and business associates who participated in the production of CRITTER CUISINE. We particularly wish to thank David Hopkins, who was with us in almost every aspect of the photography. Rick Perry and Friends were an invaluable source of inspiration and accommodation. This book would not have been published without the encouragement and collusion of John Egerton, Mac Talmadge, Chuck Mumah, Tony and Poppy Anthony, Manny Rubio, Martha Hall, Chet Sailor, Mary Alice Robinson, Chae Austin and the Pritchards, Judith, Warren and Daniel. ◆ Many thanks to Fuji for their fine film. ◆ We are grateful to our children, Jennie, Hope, Kevin, Galen and David, for participating, however unwillingly or unwittingly, in various of our culinary experiments over the years (not necessarily including those found in these pages).

Introduction

I like to refer to the place where we live as our "country home." In truth, it is our only home and not exactly in the country and not exactly in the city—more like in the suburbs of a medium-sized town. But I did grow up in the country and married a small-town boy I met at the county high school when I was a freshman and he was a junior. He went to the university and I went to the community college. My daddy didn't believe in a college education for a female who was just going to get married and stay at home to raise children and take care of a husband. Partly to stay on his good side and partly because I really enjoyed it, I did major in home economics and art education, but I took a minor in journalism (Daddy never knew about that). This turned out to be a real stroke of foresight as you will see when you turn the pages of this book. ◆ After we married, my husband got a great job with the steel wire company which had just relocated its headquarters from up north to our town. He makes a real good living for us and I don't have to work outside the home. We decided that I would make our home life my career. I took that assignment quite seriously. ◆ Everyone says our home is the prettiest in our neighborhood, thanks to me (my husband is no handyman). I combed the library for books: How to Winterize Your Home, Ten Steps to a Beautiful Lawn, All About Wallpapering and Painting, Refinishing Your Old Furniture, Decorate with Sheets—I read them all. I also took a correspondence course, Flower Arranging and Drying Flowers for Lasting Beauty. And I put all my knowledge to practical use. As you can tell, I have a great deal of energy! ◆ When the children started coming, I convinced my husband to do natural childbirth exercises with me. We used a videotape

I ordered from a copy of Parenting and You magazine that I found in the obstetrician's office. All my friends thought I was nuts, but I read all those books by Bradley, Lamaze, LeBoyer, etc., and I knew that a truly intelligent modern woman would not want to bring her babies into this world all dopey and limp limbed. It is not a normal thing for a woman to be put to sleep when she is about to be part of the greatest miracle on earth. ◆ Anyway, after the birth of our first baby, I became interested in what kind of foods he would eat when he was old enough. Then and there I decided I needed to be more informed about infant nutrition. So I picked up some books from the library, like Diet for a Small Planet and others by Euell Gibbons and Adele Davis. I started making my son's food in a blender I ordered from Penney's. He never ate a jar of store-bought baby food. ◆ I felt so good about this I thought I could do even better by him and my husband and me if I grew the vegetables and fruits that I prepared—just to be sure there were no poisonous pesticides or other chemicals on them. My husband doesn't like to work in the yard at all so I hired two of those Lorde boys (now, they **really** live in the country!) to plow up a half acre in the back of our house and then talked a neighbor's teenaged son into helping me plant and maintain a small vegetable garden and a few dwarf fruit trees and several blueberry bushes. ◆ Without going into a lot of detail here, we can say that the project grew and grew. I subscribed to Cook's Magazine, The Organic Farmer, Food and Wine. I even joined the American Institute of Wine and Food. Julia Child is a member of AIWF! I never miss "The Frugal Gourmet" on TV and I try to watch all the cooking shows available. It is amazing what one can learn by keeping one's mind receptive to new ideas. My interest in growing and preparing food became my life's work and I was ready for it. Feeding my family and friends nutritious meals that taste wonderful and look beautiful (you must know by now that I have a very artistic nature) became my consuming passion. ◆ Unfortunately, a lot of the ingredients called for in the recipes I want to prepare are not available in the grocery stores around here. But some of them I can, and do, grow myself—orange peppers, arugula, radicchio, and all the herbs I can order from the seed catalogs. If I do say so myself, our garden is a masterpiece; certainly it is unique in our area. It continues to grow both in size and in scope. ◆ However, at the outset I found myself spending more time than I had to spare keeping out the insects, possums, raccoons, etc. Since I don't want to use pesticides or needlessly kill any living creature, I put my nearly Mensa brain into gear and came up with what I think is a fabulous solution. What began as a gardener's dilemma has resulted in our book, CRITTER CUISINE. ◆ Think of this—Hindus won't eat cows, Muslims won't eat pigs, Chinese won't eat cheese. Are these so different from our own food prejudices? Would we rather starve than eat something that is considered culturally distasteful? Can I change the way the Western world looks at critters? ◆ Why, with the natural and domesticated resources within my reach, I might become the next Alice Waters. The main ingredients in CRITTER CUISINE are available to one and all, and you can use your own imagination for making the dishes appetizing and lovely; I am only your guide. Now it's up to you, dear reader, to make me a culinary star. I just know you won't let me down. Good eating to you, and remember, one man's pest is another man's pièce de résistance!

CRITTER CUISINE

ARMADILLO

◆ ◆ ◆

There is a song my husband and I just love. It's about a homesick guy who wants to go back to Texas, which he calls the home of the armadillo. Well, not exclusively. The armadillo can be found all over the Southeastern states now, and those who find themselves inundated with these burrowing, armored little creatures probably would not feel too much empathy for the singer's yearnings. ◆ We say, "If you can't beat 'em, eat 'em!" Armadillos really lend themselves to the current trendy Southwestern cuisine. I have shown you here just a few of the many ways I have learned to prepare the "Dilly."

Armadillo Asado Ahumar

◆ ◆ ◆

The armadillo roast is first parboiled, then stuffed with refried beans, jalapeño peppers and papaya. Finally it is smoked over mesquite coals. Just before it is done, add the cactus leaves to the cooker. Serve on a festive platter with strawberries and fresh-cut papayas and chayotes. These give a clear, crisp, slightly sweet taste that contrasts with the heavy smoky flavor of the meat and cacti. I love to serve the best tequila available in the pottery cups we were given by a Mexican exchange student who lived with us one summer. Oaxacan rugs from my visits to Mexico are used as table coverings and complete the South of the Border ambiance.

DILLY QUESADILLAS

◆ ◆ ◆

These quesadillas can be made from leftover roast, or you can cook parts especially for this recipe. Be sure to use a really good Monterey Jack or a mild cheddar, and the quesadillas must be made only with flour tortillas, never corn. Never use goat cheese in this recipe; if you don't believe me, try it. The three salsas in brilliant colors—golden papaya, emerald tomatillo, ruby prickly pear—make these quesadillas extraordinary.

Dilly Dip

◆ ◆ ◆

The hit of a teenage party, or any party for that matter, will be my renowned Dilly Dip. With a melon baller or a grapefruit spoon, scoop out the interior of a small- to medium-sized armadillo (depending on how much of a statement you wish to make.) This meat can be reserved for the above Dilly Quesadillas. Make your favorite cactus dip, being sure to use as many jalapeños as you dare. Mound this mixture into the prepared armadillo. Serve with crisp, crunchy corn tortilla chips and bite-sized pieces of fruit and cheese. This presentation doesn't need much embellishment. The varying patterns of armadillo shell contrasted with the colors and textures of the accompaniments say it all.

Great Balls of Fire

◆ ◆ ◆

This is a real man's dish, you know, the kind of man who doesn't eat quiche. I prefer to let the guys cook this for themselves when they are out fishing or hunting or when all the wives get together and do something that's a lot more fun and leave the husbands at home to fend for themselves.

They can make the Tabasco-butter sauce as hot as a firecracker and cool off their tastebuds with cold longnecks and raw vegetables with bleu cheese dip.

That's all I care to say about it.

BATBURGERS

◆ ◆ ◆

Halloween is our favorite neighborhood holiday. Everybody participates, putting the expected aside and indulging in the fantastic. Last year when the annual supper was held at our house, no one was expecting Batburgers. You should have heard the squeals of delight when the open-faced sandwiches were passed around along with salted home fries, lettuce, tomato and cheese—all the way!

We never could have pulled this off if there hadn't been a deluge of baby bats in the old abandoned Witt house on Walnut Mountain. Two of our children were playing around over there with some of their friends late one October afternoon and saw them swarming from the attic. They couldn't wait to get home with their idea for the supper.

The children chose glossy black china and gold and orange handmade napkins and placemats from Mexico for the table. We bobbed for apples, chewed on sugarcane and munched candy corn. A great time was had by all!

Beak and Claw Surprise

◆ ◆ ◆

And what a surprise this is—your guests will be speechless! Perhaps you will be as lucky as I was and your sister-in-law will have a few mature roosters of which she is no longer enamored. That way you will know they are as fresh as can be. I have chosen here to juxtapose the cuisine of the South and the West. Luscious warm spoon bread is made from Aunt Virginia Dare's original recipe. She entrusted this family recipe to me several years ago. She made me swear on a stack of Bibles not to divulge this treasure as long as she is alive. Sorry! Actually, I have included it in my will, just in case I go before she does. It is that good! Muscadine sauce is made with grapes from our own vines and is teamed with a chunky pepper relish that I put up in canning jars every fall.

This presentation of braised heads and feet is garnished with miniature yellow pear tomatoes, tiny pearl onions and fiery red peppers and served on a bed of newly harvested greens. My mother-in-law's sunshine yellow platter is original Fiesta. The Queen Anne's Lace is from my wild-flower garden.

I have prepared this dish for two and for two hundred. The best thing about it is that no matter how many people you entertain, a half dozen birds will be enough and you will always have leftovers to enjoy for lunch the next day.

Possums have fifty teeth, more
than any other placental mammal.
Armadillos have none, really!

BEETLE SALAD

◆ ◆ ◆

My gardens are truly beautiful, but not by accident. Hard work and diligence are required to protect the desired plants from encroaching weeds, disease, harmful insects and other pests. Of course I accomplish all of this only by natural or organic methods.

In early spring a few years ago one of our family projects produced a marvelous old-fashioned scarecrow complete with straw stuffing. With minor repairs each year he is still standing guard in the middle of the vegetable garden, although he scares nothing away. The crows actually like to perch on his outstretched arms as they munch whatever delicacies they can glean from the cabbages beneath them.

Much more effective are the amazing beetle traps that contain a sex lure, enticing the insects to come inside a container from which they cannot escape. We collect thousands of beetles over the growing season. Even my husband likes to go out in the early morning and scoop them up.

We can sometimes hear him twanging out some old George Jones lament, not a care in this world. (Since it's not often that we find something he is willing to do, we have assigned him that task and the title of "Man Who Sings with Beetles.")

It was not difficult to figure out that beetles are not only edible but also complement a great variety of foods. Since they are so plentiful at the peak of the produce season, it was only reasonable that I try them on salads made of fresh raw vegetables straight from the garden. I particularly love the iridescent green beetles on purple savoy, a feast for the color sense as well as the taste buds.

But as much as all members of our family like them, we cannot eat as many beetles as we catch, so I came up with a way of preserving them. This precipitated another family project—sun drying the beetles and storing them in antique bottles and old cricket boxes that I collect throughout the year. Nowadays all you have to say is "sun-dried" and people will line up for two city blocks to get some.

During the big holiday festivities at the end of the year I decorate the bottles with ribbons and dried flowers (which I also grow and dry myself) and present these gifts to friends and neighbors. I do attach a small card with a couple of recipes and serving suggestions, as many of the recipients haven't a clue what to do with these jewels from the garden.

Even of these may ye eat; the locust after his kind, and the bald locust after his kind, and the beetle after his kind, and the grasshopper after his kind.

Leviticus 11:22

Fisherman's Refresher

◆ ◆ ◆

Many times I have been lured on a camping trip with promises of wonderful breakfasts of freshly caught fish cooked over an open fire by the gloating fisherpersons. Just as many times I have awakened late and crawled out of my moldy tent to face several pairs of pleading hungry eyes, depending upon me to find a substitute for the ones that got away.

Now I just send my gang off on their own while I spend a leisurely weekend catching up on my reading and eating baskets of buttery croissants and homemade peach marmalade and drinking divine French roasted coffee sans grounds. (Although I don't have my own coffee bushes I buy the beans green and roast them myself. This way I know I will brew a perfect cup of coffee.)

My secret? When fishing fever strikes I make sure to pack a couple of prepared dishes for the crew to eat with their catch. (You must pretend to believe they will catch something!) Also I make sure that they take a super abundance of various baits. Then when hunger strikes before the trout does, they simply whip up a little meal of mixed baits. Red wrigglers, corn kernels and red salmon roe is an all-time favorite combination. After all, they were willing to eat a fish that had eaten the same things.

Not only is it delicious and nutritious, this dish is also a color riot that cheers them on and keeps their lines in the water. Accompanied by coleslaw and a loaf of good, sliced white bread, this meal is usually followed by a long nap and renewed optimism for "catch of the day" for the evening meal. For this they are on their own.

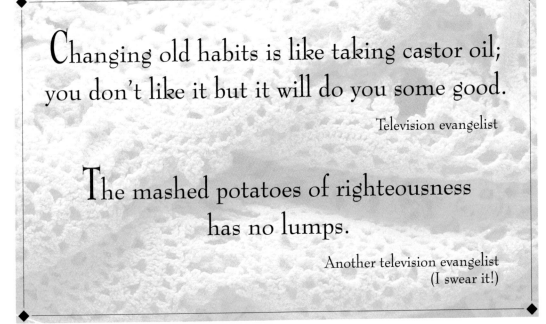

Changing old habits is like taking castor oil;
you don't like it but it will do you some good.

Television evangelist

The mashed potatoes of righteousness
has no lumps.

Another television evangelist
(I swear it!)

MIXED LIZARDS DEMI-CHAUD FROID

◆ ◆ ◆

So commonly available they are often overlooked as a nutrition source, lizards can offer quite novel innovations for everyday fare. Some are quite colorful and shapely, but others may need a little assistance to provoke appetites. Very effective is a chaud froid sauce, which provides a background for almost limitless design possibilities.

Remember, I am an artist.

A bed of fish-stock aspic provides a jewel-like base for the ornate reptiles. Carrots and dill are natural accompaniments to lizard dishes. Also quite successful is the sharp punch of cool crisp radishes. The faux stone dishes create a perfect ambiance.

Aunt Charlotte Olivia says that blue-tail lizards are to be avoided at all costs. Ingestion has been known to cause rapid and dramatic weight loss and limp tongues that hang lifelessly outside one's mouth.

MARCHING THROUGH GEORGIA

◆ ◆ ◆

A great many Northerners as well as other regionalists have discovered what a great place the South is to live. So many, in fact, that almost half the people in our neighborhood hail from north of the Mason-Dixon Line. Although I count among them some of my nearest and dearest friends it sometimes seems that a true Southern-born resident is difficult to find and is considered a curiosity by the invaders. They are always saying things like, "Now that's really Southern, isn't it?" How would I know, I've never lived anywhere else. I have nothing with which to compare it. I probably thought it was perfectly normal.

The region we live in today is resplendent with beautiful trees and other lovely flora and boasts fine homes and high-rise office buildings to rival any in the world. This is no thanks to the ancestors of the hordes who now gravitate to the warm climate and civilized pace of our ancestors.

One February when the weather was a little less than balmy, I decided we needed a boost for our spirits. So I had a party to introduce some of our Yankee friends to true Southern cuisine. Each native brought an indigenous dish she or he felt would illuminate our culture for the newcomers. The winner, hands down, was my Marching through Georgia, a reminder of that famous tourist of not so long ago, General William Tecumseh Sherman.

Various animal feet were roasted and set into whipped sweet potatoes, which resemble the red clay of Georgia. Magnolia leaves and antique lace cloths from my Great-Great-Aunt Nancy Euphrates are mementos of the glorified era immediately preceding the fiery march.

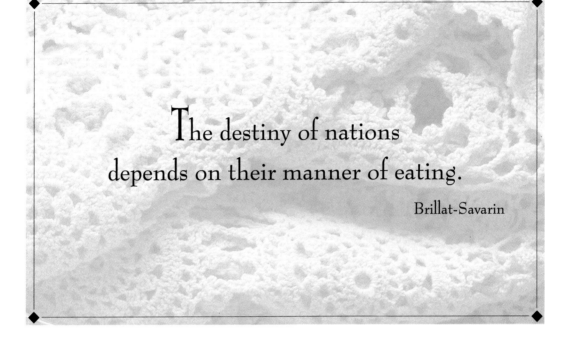

The destiny of nations
depends on their manner of eating.

Brillat-Savarin

MICE

◆ ◆ ◆

I once read that mice living in the wine cellars of France were considered quite desirable when spit roasted over a fire made with discarded old wine barrels. Well, why not? This must be a precursor to the processed entrées seen in our supermarkets today. There was your main course already marinated, or perhaps even pickled! ◆ With such a tradition to support me, I began to look with a new attitude at the scurrying little creatures in my corn patch.

Pocket Mice

◆ ◆ ◆

Those of us who are old enough to remember, with fondness, love beads and Indian block-print bedspreads were also the forerunners of the health-food craze. Most of us have lightened up a bit now and will occasionally eat cake that contains no carrots or unsulphured molasses, or bread without wheat berries. Some of us have even reintroduced meat into our diets.

This luncheon or light supper meal is a salute to the bygone days of the tie-dyed tee-shirt. It is the simple pita sandwich of tomato, avocado and the ubiquitous alfalfa sprouts updated with the addition of grilled field mice.

Our teenager likes to throw "retro" parties, and Pocket Mice is one of the most requested items at these bashes. Of course, the scene would not be complete without bunches of flowers picked from my wildflower fields. You know, "Once a flower child. . . ."

MOUSE KABOBS

◆ ◆ ◆

Sunday night suppers are eaten very leisurely at our house. Usually I just throw some chops or burgers on the grill and make a big salad with lettuces and other favorites picked by each family member from our salad garden. But once in a while we like something different.

If it is mouse kabobs we have in mind, everyone just scoops up as many mice as he or she can find, or wants to eat, while out in back picking tomatoes and lettuce. The mice are skewered with whatever other vegetables we have gathered. A charcoal fire augmented with trimmings from my herb garden permeates the kabobs with a heady earthy flavor.

FESTIVE POSSUM

◆ ◆ ◆

Possum is best if spit cooked with oak logs. The addition of persimmon wood imparts a most distinctive yet still subtle flavor to the slow-roasted meat. The possum (some people say opossum) may be stuffed with white bread and corn bread stuffing. Sage leaves and chestnuts add a festive flavor for a holiday pièce de résistance.

Possum has a special affinity for the fruits and vegetables of fall, especially persimmons, which, incidentally, are a special taste treat for the still perambulating possum. I love to experiment in my garden with pumpkins. Filled with a collard soufflé, these miniature ones make a decorative as well as a delicious vegetable dish. Corn with chopped pimentos is served in one of my antique covered casserole dishes. This particular Wedgwood bowl was given to me on my twenty-first birthday by my mother, Nancy Eugenia Malcomb. Fresh persimmons and pomegranate seeds are all you need for dessert.

Snake and Eggs in the Grass

♦ ♦ ♦

This is one of the most elegant dishes I have ever created. Visually everything seems to be in the only place it could be. How else to arrange the two sizes of garden snakes, where else to put the quail eggs, what else to bed them on but the flat garlic chives? Elegance demands simplicity, so all that is served with the main course is toasted French bread slices and a coarse mustard sauce. There is no wine that I know of to match Snake and Eggs; one must have bourbon and branch water.

For the setting I have used my mother's wedding china. The black band broken by delicate flowers is a perfect echo of the intertwined snakes.

TADPOLES

♦ ♦ ♦

If you have children and a creek, you have tadpoles. Even people living in the middle of the city are most likely in the proximity of a small stream or park pond. Every spring and summer we have quart jars all over the house filled with murky water and tadpoles at various stages of their metamorphosis into frogs. ♦ With the hundreds of tadpoles found swimming in every available water hole, you may wonder why the world is not besieged with adult frogs. Well, aside from those that die at the hands of children or other predators, many are consumed by an underground cult of tadpole devotees. Once the public realizes that they are every bit as tasty as oysters and infinitely cheaper and more available, we are going to see tadpole farms that rival the catfish farms of Mississippi. ♦ We love tadpoles on the half shell—I just use some shells we've collected at the beach since they don't come with their own. Take along horseradish, catsup and saltines on your Fourth of July picnic, and you can catch tadpoles right out of the creek, icy cold, and they couldn't be fresher. They also make a great stew that I often serve on Christmas Eve.

TADPOLE CONSOMMÉ

◆ ◆ ◆

My most frequent way of serving tadpoles is in a light vegetable consommé with vermicelli. The soup is seasoned with flat-leaf parsley, chives and a bit of lemon grass. I like to present it in our gold-banded soup dishes. Grandmother Mary Dee's heirloom crocheted tablecloth and handmade linen napkins set off the lightly etched gold-banded crystal that has been handed down in my family for four generations. The orange cosmos from my wildflower garden adds just the touch of color needed to make an inviting table setting.

A Tad Exotic

♦ ♦ ♦

When we feel like really doing something ultra, we bring out some of the finer pieces of my textile collection. This is an accumulation of flea-market finds, gifts, travel souvenirs and family heirlooms. One of my most prized pieces is this rich paisley scroll from India, enhanced here by two French black silk shawls, one with gold braid and the other with five-inch silk fringe. You cannot serve a "run-of-the-mill" meal with these extraordinary works of art.

The tadpoles are presented on decorative green leaves (just make sure the greenery you choose won't make you or the tadpoles break out in hives). Their cool taste is contrasted with two Indian condiments, chili pickle and tandoori paste. The golden glow of saffron rice blends with the warmth of the brass, stone and wooden accessories. Crisp cucumbers or tandoras (you will most likely have to grow these yourself) add welcome coolness and texture.

TOAD IN THE WHOLE

◆ ◆ ◆

This is a variation on the Bullseye or Egg in a Basket that we all enjoyed as youngsters when camping out with the Scouts. If only we had known! Toad in the Whole can be a sophisticated brunch served with a delightfully light Toadstool Omelet. What could be quicker or more elegant? It also makes an entertaining breakfast for children and picky eaters who, if they are not going to eat anyway, may as well have something to hold their interest while the rest of us enjoy our meal.

Always use day-old French or Italian bread for the toast—the toadlets need a firm bed. I like to gather mushrooms from the woods in back of our house; so far I have picked the safe ones. Some of the more exotic mushrooms are actually easy to grow in the crawl space of your basement or on logs out in the woods. You can order spores through the mail. If you must purchase yours, choose your own favorites. I find cremini or enoki to be particularly suitable and even the store-bought white ones will do, but avoid porcini and other strongly flavored fungi, as they will overpower the delicate flavor of the toadies.

A sprinkle of crushed red pepper on the omelet gives the meal just the right amount of zing. A sauté of newly harvested zucchini and tomatoes with oregano adds a nice touch of garden freshness. Pitcher plants from my pond and another of my mother-in-law's Fiesta plates add a welcoming warmth to the table.

Trot and Squeal

• • •

The Sunday following a hog killing in our neighborhood finds this lucky family the possessor of porcine treasures—the head and feet of the butchered hog. Because of the tendency to process every part of the animal, including its oink, it is something of an accomplishment to make away with these sought after "spoils," if you will.

The parts are generally roasted (indoors or out) and served up as decoratively as possible. The meat is "picked" or "pulled" as at a traditional pig roast. Pomegranates from the bushes that hedge the southwest corner of our orchard are used in the brown sugar sauce that is cooked in acorn squash halves. Bay leaves and carrots, which are stuffed into the head along with onions before it is cooked, are also used in a whimsical garnish.

This is definitely a meal to share with friends and family. We often invite guests for the whole weekend of this down-to-earth, back-to-nature experience. Good little children are given the crisp ears as special treats.

Winged Victory

◆ ◆ ◆

This dish is so much FUN!! There are innumerable ways to arrange the ears, snout and wings. I have chosen here a basically symmetrical California Nouvelle presentation using some of the contemporary china and crystal that we are beginning to acquire. I adore the idea of mixed ethnic cuisines and here I "wing" around the world to embrace Asian, African, South American, North American and Western European cultures. WHEW!

Watch your guests' eyes widen with delight when they see pig ears and snout surprisingly paired with turkey wings—who could have foreseen such a combination?

I have carried the daring even further by saucing my homemade pasta with okra and cranberry bean sauce. As one might expect after seeing my lovely orchard, the snout is served on a peach purée, but what one might not expect are the tiny banana blossoms from my patio trees adding an indescribable edge to the predominant peach flavor.

INDEX